Who's Angie?

**A Story Beginning in Abuse and Displacement,
but Ending in Triumph**

Self Help Book

by Angela Sewell

CONTENTS:

Thank You

Thank you, God. Without God nothing is possible, so I would like to thank the man above for bringing me through the storms and being with me at every turn. Everything happens for a reason and I know that the struggles I've gone through have turned me into the resilient butterfly I am today. Thank you, God for allowing me to write this book, for my blessings in the past, present, and future and for the reader of this book.

Thank *you,* dear reader for taking the time to go through this journey with me. Outlined in this book you will find not only my struggles, but my triumphant moments as well. Moreover, it is so easy to feel alone in the world today, but I hope by reading *Who is Angie?* you will feel there is someone out there who understands and feel a little less alone. I hope this book may give someone hope, empathy for others and/or compassion.

Best Wishes and Again Thank You.

❖ A.S.

Dedication

Who is Angie? Is dedicated to several inspiring, lovely people in my life, both those listed in this book and those who I have not included are equally listed in my heart. I also dedicate this book to survivors and victims of abuse whether it be mental, physical, and/ or emotional. To those who remain in the struggle I pray for you and hope the sunrises again.

For Help Call or Visit:

Domestic Violence Support | The National Domestic Violence Hotline (thehotline.org)

800.799.SAFE (7233)

National Hotlines (victimconnect.org)

https://victimconnect.org/get-help/victimconnect-chat/

855-4-Victim (855-484-2486)

Support Group For Maryland Crime Victims + Family + Friends (mdcrimevictims.org)

301-952-0063 or 1-877-VICTIM-1

INTRO: SERENITY PRAYER

God, give me grace to accept with serenity

the things that cannot be changed,

Courage to change the things

which should be changed,

and the wisdom to distinguish

the one from the other.

Living one day at a time,

Enjoying one moment at a time,

Accepting hardship as a pathway to peace,

Taking, as Jesus did,

This sinful world as it is,

Not as I would have it,

Trusting that You will make all things right,

If I surrender to Your will,

So that I may be reasonably happy in this life,

And supremely happy with You forever in the next.

Amen.- Reinhold Niebuhr

Ch. 1 AUNT SOPHIE- THE VALIENT MOTHER

"Whoever receives one child such as this in my name, receives me; and whoever receives me, receives not me but the One who sent me." (Mark 9: 36-37)

In the midst of Edmonson and Normandy Avenue, an urban backdrop riddled by crime, drugs, racial injustice, and prostitution, lived a vivacious Samaritan whose lady bug décor-adorned home contrasted the climate surrounding it. This home with its canine guard, a Doberman Pinscher named Candy (whose demeanor when in protection mode was quite contrary to the sweetness of her name), was the safe haven that I would grow accustomed to on and off for the next seven years.

It takes a phenomenal kind of woman to adopt and rear children, children whose lives had been darkened by misfortune. From adopting a young, pregnant immigrant girl, who escaped the horrors of sex trafficking to adopting myself, a lost, multiracial child and an active victim of neglect and sexual abuse, Aunt Sophie was an unconventional hero and a beacon of light in the lives of several youths.

Kind, loving, just, stoic, motherly are an understatement of the adjectives that describe sweet Aunt Sophie. Aunt Sophie stood at 5'7"with a sun kissed brown complexion, luscious black locks, and an athletic build. She was of Native American and African American heritage. I arrived at Aunt Sophie's door in tattered garb, one bag in hand: four pairs of undergarments, four pairs of pants, three shirts and a weathered toothbrush, and even still the smell of sweet potato pie, collard greens and oyster pancakes gave me comfort. I stepped into the home unaware of the pertinent love and guidance I would receive from my new guardian.

The French styled living room draped in plastic of Aunt Sophie's transformed into a playground, as it protected us from the tough streets of Edmonson village in the early 1980s. By "us" I refer to my second cousin Agatha Combs and her children my first cousins: Cassidy, Eric, and Jerry Combs, who were also residents of the spacious row home. Agatha Combs, the mother was a stern, intimidating, but at the same time loving woman. Her daughter the oldest of the three, Cassidy was someone I aspired to be. She was a fashion-forward, brown skin, tall, medium built, curvy girl who was tough, hardworking, and driven. Eric was the sly one of the group. He was lean and energetic, with a dazzling smile (which contributed to his mischievous ways). Jerry the youngest was doe-eyed and the peacemaker of the group. Oftentimes, the four of us kids would sneak out and visit Trudy our neighbor across the street when we weren't busy watching pro-wrestling on tv or playing some inventive game in the living room. Cassidy, Eric, Jerry and I got along for the most part, but the times where we did not get along were brutal. They would pick on, make fun of, and prank me. At times they would call me "white girl" as an insult and bully me by pulling my hair and insulting my proper speech. It definitely began to affect my self-esteem. Regardless of the ongoing tormenting, Aunt Sophie was always there, cape in tow to pick up the pieces. She offered comforting words and a tender embrace. Still finally the day came when I had had enough. I have always loved the creamy, rich taste of Breyers vanilla bean ice cream. One day, however; my cousins enticed me with the sweet dessert. I took a big scoop of the ice cream an immediately regretted it. The cousins had filled an empty container of Breyers with an off-brand ice cream and mixed pepper into it causing my eyes to tear and my mouth to become inflamed. I was over all the teasing, pranks, and name calling and demanded out of Aunt Sophie's house. My stepfather retrieved me, birth mother in the passenger seat---drunk and strung out on various pills. I would quickly regret my departure from Aunt Sophie's. I would grow to miss Aunt Sophie's hearty homecooked meals, words of wisdom, Biblical stories, vivid tales of her prime years living in Hawaii, and powerful prayers.

Ch 2. Louie- The Impeccable Stepfather

"Do not be overcome by evil, but overcome evil with good." Romans 12:21

Louie, my lifesaver, my breath of fresh air, my stand-in dad was a golden-brown complexion, statuesque hard-working man. He was the definition of "a provider" always working two jobs at a time to make ends meet. Sometimes I would go with him to a night cleaning job, as one of his job titles was maintenance man. He'd work diligently and let me vacuum the floors. To this day I still find a certain peace in vacuuming the floors. Although he wasn't my natural father, he took on the role with no hesitation. Every Friday he'd take me, my younger sister, and my baby brother to the local fast-food restaurant to get fish sandwiches and hot fudge sundaes. My stepfather was also a religious man so he'd invent fun gospel songs and take us kids to church on Sundays when he could. Nonetheless, despite Louie's kind nature, the days that followed my departure from Aunt Sophie's were filled with torture. Because of the abusive nature of my birth mother as a result of her illicit drug and alcohol abuse, I was forced to gain a thick skin in order to combat the tumultuous environment. At the tender age of 10 began my speedy adultification. I would witness a lifestyle no child should ever be subject to.

Watching television became my escape. Shows like "Three's Company", "Family Ties", and "Who's the Boss" would oftentimes help me drown out not only the external but the internal noise. I longed for the healthy relationships displayed by those television families, - the happy times, the love filled, comedic situations that my own life lacked. To say reality paled in comparison to those sitcoms would be a vast understatement.

Unlike Elyse Keaton, the traditional, loving, upbeat mother from "Family Ties", birth mother in contrast was volatile, abusive, and neglectful like the maternal "figure" from "Mommy Dearest". Her abusive episodes directly and unfortunately affected Louie my undeserving stepfather. This would ultimately lead to their divorce later in life. She would drink toxic levels of liquor and become angry. Then she would throw any object she could find and scream obscenities. Louie and I were always on the receiving end of the insults and the hurled china. One time in particular, I had escaped to my alternate reality via tv, when I heard the sound of glass dinnerware shattering against the walls of her bedroom. By the time I got to birth mother's room I found her with a butcher knife at Louie's neck. Survival mode kicked in and I sprang into action knocking birth mother away from Louie. That night would be the last straw for Louie and he would not soon return to the house. After Louie made his departure the days seemed darker. He would occasionally check in on me, my sister, and brother, but his presence in the household was definitely missed.

Ch. 3 Gary- The Protective Brother

Gary, birth mother's first born was another savior of mine. His warm brown skin, brilliant smile, and wavy hair gave him resemblance to a young Usher. He stood at 6'3," with a slender build which was expectant of the military man. Gary possessed a matter-of-fact attitude and was kind and generous to say the least. Although I didn't always see him because he lived with his paternal grandmother, Mrs. Ruth, his role and guidance in my life was extremely impactful. Bright eyed and youthful with a healthy dose of skepticism were also his marking traits. At the age of 17 he began working at the local market. Sometimes I would have to wait for Gary after work and he would always greet me with a warm smile and a French Vanilla milkshake. Gary had a path planned for himself: to make enough money to afford a car and then to soldier off to the military. I enjoyed spending time with Gary up until he left for the military and got stationed in Hawaii. Once again, I felt lost and alone, but every time I missed my older brother 6 months would roll around and a package would arrive with Hawaiian garb and luau materials. I would put on my grass skirt and lei and dance around happily. It would be 2 years until I saw my big bro again. Unfortunately, though, the day Gary came back would not be joy filled. While he was away in the Navy, Gary would send his military checks back home trusting that birth mother would put them into a savings account. However, true to her greedy and selfish tendencies, birth mother had spent the $20,000 Gary had accumulated over 2 years on a fancy new car. Words were exchanged when my brother returned home and he stormed out of the house devastated. My heart broke for him.

I assume the guilt of stealing money from her child took a toll as birth mother began drinking at least a fifth of vodka and a 24 pack of malt liquor a day. The verbal and physical abuse against me would continue and she would drink well into 9 months of her pregnancy with my new brother.

Sooner than later though a guardian angel in my neighborhood who had been (unknowingly to any of us) watching the house reported Birth Mother to the officials for neglect. My baby brother had been taken away previously by family members, but my sister and I were constantly left to our own devices. Social workers and advocates began coming to my school to interview me during lunch and recess. When I told my birth mother, she had the audacity to say "keep quiet or they will lock me up." She threatened me into withholding the truth. I was used to these threats. This was the same conniving, wickedness that prompted me to fool officials by taking her weekly urine test. Nonetheless, despite my birth mother trying to evade the authorities, my absentees and the fact that my sister and I often came to school in the same clothes several days a week, was hard to hide. The day came that I was pulled out of school only to have an interview with a social worker and a child advocate. In a small dim-lit room where the atmosphere was similar to a police interrogation, Birth Mother and I were questioned. After noticing my nervousness and shaky composure they separated us. I can remember

Birth Mother yelling "Remember I'm your mother!" as she was led away. This was her way of trying to control me and an attempt to shake me up. The moment Birth Mother was out of the room I felt safe. I don't know what came over me, but the next thing I know I was revealing what was really going on. I revealed the gross neglect, the uninhabitable living conditions, and the child endangerment I'd faced. Once the 24-hour investigation was complete, I was immediately removed from Birth Mother's custody. My sister was sent to live with her father, but my destiny was different as my dad had passed on. On June 11, 1992, red bag in hand containing my few belongings, I stood in the social services office late at night with a feeling of devastation hovering over my head. I knew my living conditions were less than ideal, but it still was a hard pill to swallow leaving the place I referred to as home. It was decided that night I would go to the home of Mrs. Bertha Knight.

Ch. 4 Bertha Knight- My Knight in Shining Motherhood

A rancher style, one-level home which stretched for many acres awaited me. In it lived a mother of three, a light skinned woman with big beautiful exotic hazel eyes, tapered curly mahogany hair, an air of sophistication, and a dazzling smile that could light up the darkest night. Although she was short in stature, Mrs. Bertha Knight's personality stood at least 6 feet tall. I was her first foster child, but she would go on to foster for over 40 more years. She was extremely loving. I thank God to have met this woman.

My first night at casa de Knight I had the best sleep of my life. The transition from my old life to the new life in Bertha Knight's care was seamless. She took me shopping, made the best breakfasts, she made sure I aspired to higher education. I can accredit this lovely woman alone with helping me obtain scholarships to attend college. Mrs. Knight showed me the ropes and played an instrumental part in my teenage years.

When the Knight's had their annual family picnic, I felt extremely nervous. Even though Mrs. Knight and her three daughters made me feel welcome, I still felt a sense of isolation. This immediate family was accepting, but I was anxious to know if the extended family would mirror the sentiment. For a while I hung back by myself. Mrs. Bertha took notice and immediately reassured me we'd be melded together for life. She truly took me in as one of her own. To this day I am still in contact with this precious soul. Unfortunately, though, my time at this place of solace would much like the other joys in my life be cut far too short. 60 days after I arrived at Mrs. Knight's I would be sent to live with my big brother, Gary and his new wife.

Ch. 5 Gary- Part II

The authorities had located my brother Gary and sent me to live with him and his new wife. Mallory, Gary's wife resembled Peppa of salt n Peppa. Her skin was warm cocoa brown and paid homage to her dark brown locks. A 5'2", drowsy eyed, ratchet, but classy woman who was a true hustler is what my sister-in-law could be described as. She wore her hair in a French roll with finger waves and rod set going down the side. She was a hairstylist so never was there a strand of hair out of place. Mallory gravitated towards 90s styled fashion.

Unfortunately, though, my brother's now ex-wife would go from free spirited, go getter to a hardened gold digger, but before going into that let me backtrack.

I was fond of Mallory until the time came where she turned on me, presumably because of events (by no fault of mine) that transpired in her marriage. Her ambitious nature and "ready to take on the world" attitude became compromised when she learned of infidelity that transgressed in her marriage. When she learned her husband had cheated on her with an exotic, dark haired Dominican woman (who was also married) from the local grocery store (where they all worked) she snapped. The way she found out was devastating to say the least. Gary, Mallory, and Mallory's mother, Tammie all worked at the same grocery store. Gary's mother-in-law overheard a conversation between my brother and his mistress. Gary had been unfaithful to his wife for some time. Then one day a little boy came in the market with a strong resemblance to my brother. Tammie informed Gary that if he did not tell her daughter, then she would do the job herself. Gary withheld the information until he finally cracked under pressure and awoke in a cold sweat in the middle of night to break the heart wrenching news. The situation was made worse when a pregnant Mallory waddled into work the following week to pick up her check. She witnessed Gary talking to the mistress and confronted them both with a slew of angry insults and malicious threats. However, this wouldn't be my brother's last transgression.

The problems in the marriage escalated quickly, so by the time I was sent to live with the couple tensions were at an all-time high. Mallory began taking her misguided anger out on me. Checks from the state that were meant to be spent on my wellbeing she would take and treat herself to luxuries. A deluxe new car, a face lift for her home, were just a few things my money for food and clothing were spent on. She also was mean spirited and short tempered with me. I felt reduced to Cinderella, as my "evil stepmother" forced me into a subdivision of the laundry room in the basement- a closet if you will. I would go on to babysit her kids and neglect my own social life and school work. I also would be forced to claim ownership of an ever-growing list of chores piled on without hesitation. My brother, with his guilt of his crimes against the marriage, stayed out of it and did very little to stop my mistreatment. One event particularly stood out to me. It was Winter- Christmas time, Mallory had had it up to her ears with Gary's continuous betrayal of their vows. I remember this day like it was yesterday. The woman took my neatly wrapped Christmas presents (which had been purchased with my own money) and launched them out the door into the snow. She went on a manic episode screaming for me to get out of the house. She was constantly filling my brother's head with untruths about me in order to falsely justify her claims and gain support in kicking me out of the house. She called me "hot in the pants" and practically claimed I was stealing her money--my settlement money! Instead of dealing with her own marital problems she found a slight, sick comfort in making my life a living Hell. That frigid winter day my brother found me outside and tried desperately to reason with Mallory, to no avail. I could already sense the disappointing outcome before my brother relayed the message "My wife says you have to leave. You're coming between our marriage." In that moment I felt defeated. I felt my brother should stand up to his wife, have a backbone. I felt lost once again, but simultaneously I felt a sense of relief.

Ch- 6 Leaving the System- My Own Hero

After leaving my brother's house I was sent back to Mrs. Knight's. I was ecstatic to return to my former foster mother's home. Who says lightning doesn't strike twice? For a second time in my adolescent life, I was to able experience the loving warmth of my former foster mother's home. I was welcomed back with open arms and for a moment felt at piece with the way things were. To go through Hell and back was almost worth it to end up in this place where the grass literally and figuratively was greener. After years of emotional and physical turmoil things were starting to look up. I stayed with Mrs. Knight for a few more years right up until my 18th birthday when it was time for me to go out into the world alone. At 18 years of age, I left the system. For a while there would be more struggle. I still had major life lessons to learn and self-love to obtain.

I eventually picked up two jobs and moved in with my first serious boyfriend all while attending college. I lived with Troy in a two-bedroom apartment. The second bedroom was occupied by another couple, John and Linda. Troy was much older than I. The relationship had its ups, but the majority of it consisted of downs. At that time, one of my jobs was a bartender. As we all know working as a bartender entails serving drinks to sometimes overly friendly customers. Men would flirt with me and Troy was not a fan of that aspect of the job. This and the fact that I resumed picking up sporadic modeling gigs were things that drove Troy to resent me. In the beginning of our relationship, he took me out to fancy dinners and treated me to nice gifts, but this all took a downward shift once the bartending and modeling came into play. He became possessive and spiteful. He spewed words of hatred and became physically violent. Linda befriended me and ask why I tolerated the awful treatment. Maybe it was because of years and physical, emotional, and verbal torment at the hands of my birth mother. Maybe I had become accustomed to the pain and it seemed inevitable. I continued to put up with the abuse until finally I could take no more. It was time for a change. I had to stop believing I deserved to be treated that way. I deserved real love, honor, and respect. What I didn't deserve was someone putting their hands on me and draining me both mentally and physically. I had to get out, be on my own, and find my path in life without this man. So, I took my things and left in the middle of the night and never looked back.

I continued on to college and obtained my degrees. I took the lessons of the people I loved most and then finally life began to get a little sweeter. I started a job in my field and went on to start a nonprofit, *Helping People.* I would go on to help victims of emotional and physical trauma and neglect. I find and collect resources for them, mentor youth, act as a life coach, and help people with job searches and students with earning service-learning hours for school. I've walked in the shoes of the underserved and it was not an easy walk, so I want to give back as much as I can. My life is still a work in progress, but I am proud to say I've come a long way. This is nowhere near the end of my story, but just the beginning. I pray that everyone who has gone through the turbulent waters of life finds in God a lifejacket and gets a chance to rise up from the ashes.

❖ **Always invest in yourself.** There is no investment more crucial than investing in yourself. This is also the investment with the biggest payoff. Whether it be by education, self-help, mental health. Always stay focused and bet on you.

❖ **Choose your friends wisely.** Only let people who are a part of your peace in your circle. Surround yourself with positive and uplifting people. Protecting your energy is critical.

❖ **Trust Your Instinct.** What is something lions, good mothers, and successful investors have in common? They all trust their instincts. If it doesn't feel right don't do it simple as that. Your inner voice speaks, so make sure you listen.

❖ **Be careful with advice- giving and receiving.** Not all advice should be adhered to. If you are given advice consider the source. Is this someone you admire? Aspire to be like? Shares similar values? If the answer is "no" to these questions you probably should apply their advice with a grain of salt. But the advice of someone you do not aspire to be like can also be helpful; you may find it helpful as you can consider it the what-not-to-do advice. Also, on advice, be careful with what you give out. Think what effect it may have on the receiver and consider how the receiver will translate it.

❖ **Find a trade or go to college.** Not everyone shares the same path to success some people are destined to go to college, others aren't. What you should consider is what is best for you. Education is key and going to an accredited university can be extremely helpful, but if a trade school is more conducive to your life's goals follow that path. I do believe learning should be lifelong, so just because school ends you should never stop learning and flourishing your mind. I also want to add never let anyone tell you what you should or shouldn't do in regards to what career path you choose. If your dreams are "too big" to someone follow them anyway. Work hard and you will achieve success.

❖ **Travel the world, make list, set goals.**

❖ **Always believe in yourself even when others don't.** The world is full of naysayers, Debbie Downers, and Negative Nancy. Don't let the pessimists steal your optimism. Just because some people choose to see the downside in themselves in others try not to be affected by it. You can do anything you set your mind to.

@theartistellephotos

This is only the beginning. Lookout for the follow-up book. Thank you for your support and please support Helping People Nonprofit Organization (Baltimore, MD). This organization aims to aid and connect with the underserved community by helping them find jobs, resources, and distributing charitably donated items (when available).

Need Help?- Resources

Self-Help Stuff That Works | HealthyPlace

Inter Dependence Homepage | HealthyPlace

Find Support Groups | Mental Health America (mhanational.org)

Save a Child's Life - Donate Today | Covenant House

Home - St. Vincent de Paul of Baltimore (vincentbaltimore.org)

https://mdfoodbank.org/

NIMH » Child and Adolescent Mental Health (nih.gov)

Teen Mental Health: Facts & Statistics (adolescentwellnessacademy.com)

Maryland Food Pantries | Food Banks, Food Pantries, Food Assistance in Maryland (foodpantries.org)

A Real Mom:
Emotional, yet the rock.
Tired, but keeps going.
Worried, but full of hope.
Impatient, yet patient.
Overwhelmed, but never quits.
Amazing, even though doubted.
Wonderful, even in the chaos.
Life Changer, every single day.
- Rachel Martin

lessonslearnedinlife.com

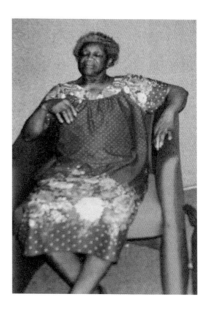

"Cause I can sit down with schollars, stand up with Thugs or Ascend on them both"

- a goddess

Made in the USA
Middletown, DE
12 May 2021